Taekwondo FOR KIDS

Y.H. Park

TUTTLE Publishing

Tokyo | Rutland, Vermont | Singapore

About Tuttle
"Books to Span the East and West"

Our core mission at Tuttle Publishing is to create books which bring people together one page at a time. Tuttle was founded in 1832 in the small New England town of Rutland USA Vermont . Our fundamental values remain as strong today as they were then—to publish best-in-class books informing the English-speaking world about the countries and peoples of Asia. The world has become a smaller place today and Asia's economic cultural and political influence has expanded yet the need for meaningful dialogue and information about this diverse region has never been greater. Since 1948 Tuttle has been a leader in publishing books on the cultures arts cuisines languages and literatures of Asia. Our authors and photographers have won numerous awards and Tuttle has published thousands of books on subjects ranging from martial arts to paper crafts. We welcome you to explore the wealth of information available on Asia at **www.tuttlepublishing.com**.

Published by Tuttle Publishing, an imprint of Periplus Editions (HK) Ltd.

www.tuttlepublishing.com

Library of Congress Cataloging-in-Publication Data

Park, Yeon Hwan.
Taekwondo for kids / Y. H. Park—1st. ed.
48 p. : col. ill. ; 29 cm.
ISBN 978-0-8048-3631-9
1. Tae kwon do—Juvenile literature. 2. Karate for children—Juvenile literature. I. Title.
GV1114.9.P353 2005
796.815'3—dc22 2004017227

IMPORTANT NOTE TO READERS:
Training in the martial arts involves physical exertion, movements, and actions that can cause injury to you or others. Because the physical activities in this book may be too strenuous for some readers, you should check with a physician before you start your training. If you are ever in doubt about how to proceed or about whether a practice is safe for you, consult with a martial arts professional before proceeding.

Illustrations by Stephanie Tok
Design by Kathryn Sky-Peck

DISTRIBUTED BY

North America, Latin America, and Europe
Tuttle Publishing
Airport Business Park
364 Innovation Drive
North Clarendon, VT 05759-9436
Tel: 1 (802) 773-8930
Fax: 1 (802) 773-6993
info@tuttlepublishing.com
www.tuttlepublishing.com

Japan
Tuttle Publishing
Yaekari Building, 3rd Floor
5-4-12 Osaki
Shinagawa-ku
Tokyo 141 0032
Tel: (81) 3 5437-0171
Fax: (81) 3 5437-0755
sales@tuttle.co.jp
www.tuttle.co.jp

Asia Pacific
Berkeley Books Pte. Ltd.
61 Tai Seng Avenue #02-12
Singapore 534167
Tel: (65) 6280-1330
Fax: (65) 6280-6290
inquiries@periplus.com.sg
www.periplus.com

First edition
21 20 19 18 10 9 8 7 6 5 4 1804EP
Printed in Hong Kong

CONTENTS

one

WHAT IS TAEKWONDO?

Would you like to learn taekwondo, and perhaps one day become a black belt? If so, you're not alone. Hundreds of thousands of young people across the nation are jumping, punching, kicking, shouting, and thinking in healthy new ways as they try to meet this goal. As these kids advance in taekwondo, they are becoming better people, stronger, more confident, and able to do things they never imagined!

An important part of taekwondo training is understanding the history of this martial art. Knowing how taekwondo started will help you understand why the masters and grandmasters—both those of the past and the present ones—are treated with such respect.

Taekwondo is the most popular martial art in the world–over fifty million people practice it!

THE HISTORY OF TAEKWONDO

Taekwondo is a Korean martial art with a long and interesting history. Taekwondo, which is best known for its amazing kicks, began more than 2000 years ago, around 50 B.C. We know this because archaeologists have found pictures of people practicing taekwondo stances, blocks, and punches on the ceiling of an ancient royal tomb in Korea, called the Muyong-Chong.

Long ago, Korea was divided into three kingdoms: Silla, Koguryo, and Baekche. The same people who eventually united Korea were also the people who spread an early form of taekwondo. These people were known as the Hwarang, which means "flowering youth." They were young warriors from royal families who underwent a great deal of physical, cultural, and philosophical training to become an elite class of knights. The Hwarang were taught Subak, which was a very early form of taekwondo that focused on kicks. The young warriors added new moves to Subak, including punches, and renamed the art Tae Kyon. The Hwarang spread their fighting arts, along with Buddhism, to the island of Japan. Some people think that the Hwarang may even have inspired the samurai culture in Japan. Either way, it is clear that from the start taekwondo was not just about kicking and punching, but also about acting honorably and respectfully.

In 1909, almost 2000 years after the Hwarang introduced Buddhism and Tae Kyon to Japan, the Japanese invaded Korea. They stayed in control of the country for thirty-six years. During this time, the Korean people were not allowed to practice Tae Kyon or other forms of Subak. You might think that since they were not allowed to practice Subak, it just died out. Not so! Instead, it spread like never before, and people went to Buddhist temples in secret to practice Subak.

STYLES

When Korea was set free from the Japanese in 1945, Subak began to spread even more. However, there were many different styles—called kwans—being practiced. Some of the kwans were Moo Duk Kwan, Chung Do Kwan, Yun Moo Kwan, and Ji Do Kwan. Although they had a lot in common, the kwans all did some things a little differently. There was no single way of bowing, warming up, punching, kicking, or competing. Sometimes the masters of one kwan did not get along with the masters of others. This made it difficult for there to be a single taekwondo community.

In the 1950s, all the masters got together and decided to unite the kwans. As you can imagine, this was a very difficult task. Each master was used to teaching his students in a different way, and it took many years for all the masters to come to an agreement. Even then, however, the masters were still divided into two groups. One group, lead by General Hong Hi Choi, became the Korea Taekwondo Association, and later the International Taekwondo Federation (ITF). The other group, led by Dr. Un Yong Kim, became the World Taekwondo Federation (WTF). The main difference between the groups is that the ITF focuses on self-defense techniques, while the WTF focuses more on competition.

Martial arts are not just styles of fighting; they are also philosophies for living honorably.

While these two groups may have slightly different ways of teaching taekwondo, they are both devoted to increasing the popularity of this martial art. Thanks in large part to the efforts of Dr. Un Yong Kim, taekwondo was a demonstration sport in the 1988 Olympics in Seoul, Korea. Today it is an official sport in the Pan American Games and the Olympic Games. And there are Junior Olympics held every year for kids just like you! Dr. Un Yong Kim and thousands of other masters are working hard to make taekwondo as popular around the world as other sports.

The WTF's new president is Dr. Chung Won Choue. He has expert leadership and vision and is looking for a new taekwondo movement in the world.

WHY SHOULD I LEARN TAEKWONDO?

If you work hard and take your taekwondo training seriously, you will start to see some amazing benefits, starting from your first day at the taekwondo school, or *dojang*. Among these are:

- *More confidence*: Taekwondo teaches you how to protect and defend yourself and others, how to act responsibly and make good decisions, and how to stay in control of your emotions and do the right thing. As you learn each of these things, you will become much more confident. This means that you will feel proud of yourself because you know that you are working hard and learning very important skills.

- *Better coordination*: The training in taekwondo is very strict and specific—this means that everyone will be expected to perform the kicks, blocks, and stances in exactly the same way, and you will have to practice until you can do them right. Because of this, you will find yourself being much more careful in all your movements, which will give you much better coordination.

- *Strength of character*: Practicing taekwondo will give you strength of character. This means that you will feel yourself becoming a better person as you live by the philosophies you're being taught. You will know how to do the right thing, how to behave with honor, and how to make others proud of you.

- *Thinking independently*: Taekwondo also teaches you to think independently. This means being able to decide what is right and wrong, and to act in a way that is right, without having to ask a grown-up for help. If, for instance, your friends want you to try something bad, you must be able to say no to them. This is sometimes hard, but training in taekwondo will give you the confidence you need to make and carry out the decisions you feel are right. Taekwondo will teach you that you know more about right and wrong than you may think.

Words to Know

Taekwondo: This means "way of the foot and fist." But taekwondo is not just a style of fighting, it's also a philosophy for life.

Dojang: A taekwondo school

two

GETTING READY FOR TAEKWONDO

If you have to wear a uniform to school, or know someone who does, you may think that wearing a uniform to taekwondo class will be a drag. However, the uniform you wear to the dojang carries a lot of history and is meant to help you get into your role as a taekwondo student. When you see someone—whether in real life, on TV, or in the movies—practicing taekwondo in their white uniform, you get a sense that this person is someone who is serious about his or her martial art. Wearing the uniform helps you feel like a serious taekwondo practitioner. Not only that, the uniform unites all students, from beginners to the most advanced. When you're in a room full of white uniforms, you will feel like you're part of a big family.

WHAT YOU SHOULD WEAR

When you begin taekwondo, you will wear a white belt and a uniform, called a *dobuk* in Korean. Dobuks are made up of pants and a jacket. The pants have either a drawstring waist or an elastic waist. If your pants have a drawstring waist, be sure that you tie them securely—but not too tightly. You'll need to move freely in your uniform, so your pants must fit comfortably.

The dobuk jacket comes in two different styles—one with a deep V-neck opening, which you slip over your head, and one that ties in the front. Be sure to find out which style your school uses. Also, it may take you a while to feel comfortable in your jacket because it will be big and loose, so you might want to wear a white T-shirt underneath it, especially if you get cold. The belt is tied over the dobuk at the waist and holds everything together.

> **Words to Know**
>
> *Sabumnim:* Your taekwondo instructor
>
> *Dobuk:* The taekwondo uniform

HOW TO TIE THE BELT

To tie your belt correctly, first fold the belt in half so that you can find the center. Place the center of the belt on your belly button and wrap your belt around your waist two times. Make sure that one of the belt straps is underneath the other, all the way around. Tug on the ends of the straps so that they're even. Cross the straps over each other, so that they make an "X." Tuck the left strap up through the other layers around your waist. Next, fold the right strap in half so

Taekwondo Tip

Tying the belt is a very important part of taekwondo. Your midsection, where the belt is tied, is your center of gravity—*tanjun* in Korean—and therefore is a key part of your body. By tying your belt carefully and precisely, you are showing respect toward your tanjun.

that it makes a loop. Now bring the left strap down in front of the loop. Pull the end of the left strap up through the loop, and at the same time tug on the end of the right strap so that your knot will be tight. When you are finished, both straps should hang at the same length.

WHAT THE DIFFERENT BELT COLORS MEAN

When taekwondo was first practiced, there were no differences in rank; everyone just wore a white belt, which was there to hold up their pants and didn't mean anything. The more someone practiced, the dirtier his belt became. The sign of an experienced taekwondo student was a really grimy belt. Today, there are different belt colors that come before the black belt. Just as in the past, the darker the belt is, the more experience the student has. Your belt is therefore very important. It shows everyone how much you know, and so it would be silly to wash your belt. In ancient times, that would have been like washing away all you had learned about taekwondo! (However, you can—and should—wash your dobuk and keep it clean.)

Nowadays, the different color belts represent different levels of experience. However, don't be fooled into thinking that all black belts have the same amount of experience, or that once you become a black belt you will know as much as your taekwondo instructor. Becoming a black belt is only the beginning for those who are serious about taekwondo—there's always more to learn and many different ways to improve.

Before you reach the black belt, the colored belts represent grades of knowledge, called *gups* in Korean. A white belt is a ninth gup, and a first gup is a red and black belt (or a red belt, depending on the belt colors used by your dojang). Once you become a black belt, your level of skill and knowledge is measured not in gups, but in *dans*, or degrees. Someone who just earned their first black belt will be a first dan. A second dan is someone who has two years of taekwondo training after receiving the black belt, and a third dan has had three years of training after reaching second dan. In order to become a *sabumnim*—taekwondo instructor—you must be a fifth dan, which means that you've put in at least fifteen years of training after becoming a black belt! Perhaps now you understand why your taekwondo teacher is to be treated with such respect; it takes a great deal of hard work and dedication to become a sabumnim.

Belt Colors

While some dojangs may have a slightly different order of colors, they will all start with the white belt and end with the black belt.

WHITE You begin with a white belt to symbolize purity (in other words, you don't know much about taekwondo yet).

YELLOW Once you pass your first belt test, you will become a yellow belt.

ORANGE You are beginning to learn and perform more complex moves.

GREEN Your techniques are getting better and better, and you can perform the basics well.

BLUE You are now practiced in the basics as well as in *poomse* (forms) and sparring.

PURPLE Congratulations! You've passed the midpoint and you're on your way to becoming a black belt. You will need to work even harder now, and your instructor will expect more from you.

RED You have now mastered the basics and can help teach beginning students who are struggling. Your new belt color signifies increased responsibility.

BROWN By now you have probably been practicing taekwondo for a long time. Your brown belt is a symbol of your hard work and dedication, as well as your increased abilities.

RED & BLACK You are now just one belt test from becoming a black belt! Everyone who sees your red and black belt will know that you are an advanced taekwondo student, and they will treat you with great respect.

BLACK You are a black belt! You have reached a very high goal, and you should be proud of yourself. You have displayed a tremendous amount of perseverance and an indomitable spirit. But remember, this is only the beginning–you can get better at taekwondo your whole life!

BLACK BELTS

Being a black belt is a great honor. However, it is also a responsibility. When you become a black belt, others in your school and outside it will think of you as a very important person. You will have accomplished something great, and people will try to copy your behavior. This means that you must always act in an honorable way and make your taekwondo master proud. If this sounds like a lot, don't worry; your instructor is not only a teacher but also your friend. He will be there to guide you as you get better and better in taekwondo, and when you have questions—about life in or out of the taekwondo school—he will be there to help.

Remember, becoming a first dan black belt is only the beginning. There is still a great deal to learn and a lot of fun to be had in the process.

If you are under sixteen but have met the requirements for becoming a black belt, you will be referred to as a junior black belt. This just means that your degrees are called *pooms* instead of dans.

three THE DOJANG

As we mentioned earlier, dojang is the Korean word for taekwondo school. If you're serious about learning taekwondo, you'll probably spend a lot of time at the dojang and with your sabumnim, so be sure to choose a dojang that you feel comfortable with. Not all dojangs will look the same, but let's go over some of the things you can probably expect to find there.

DESCRIPTION

All dojangs will consist of a large open room, usually with a hardwood floor but sometimes with a padded or carpeted floor. There will be separate changing rooms for boys and girls, and maybe even a separate room where you should leave your backpack and shoes. There usually won't be many decorations in the room, though each dojang will probably have a Korean flag and your nation's flag on the wall. There may also be mirrors or some training equipment around and possibly trophies on display.

Whether your dojang is big or small, modern or traditional, there are rules of behavior that they all share.

RULES AND ETIQUETTE

Your dojang is a special place, and you should think of it as your second home. Because it is the place where you learn taekwondo, you must always treat it with great respect. You should never run around inside the dojang, or yell or be rowdy. You should always listen to your sabumnim, as well as to the students who are more advanced than you. But these are just the general rules. Let's go over some of the rules a bit more closely.

The first thing you must do upon entering the dojang—even before you bow—is to take off your shoes. This is because you will practice in bare feet, and you don't want to track in dirt and small rocks that might cut up your feet while you're training! The floor is kept very clean. It takes a lot of hard work to make sure that you and the other students have a clean, safe surface to practice on, so be sure to keep your shoes off and not to bring in anything that might make a mess, such as food or drink. If there isn't a place to store food or drinks at the dojang, keep them in your backpack—that way other students won't accidentally uncover them or knock them over, which could cause a big mess.

When you line up for class, be sure to leave plenty of space between yourself and the students around you. The rows should all be neat and even. This is important for two different reasons. The first reason is that

Training Tip

Your dojang is more than a gym–it is where you learn taekwondo, and therefore a place of great respect. You must be on your very best behavior in the dojang.

lining up in straight rows helps you stay centered and focused—try concentrating on your moves when you see students jumbled all around you! The second reason is that staying in neat rows ensures that you won't accidentally hit another student while practicing.

Be sure to listen carefully to your sabumnim and to the students who are more advanced than you. You will need to know how to do each move exactly; otherwise, you will have a very hard time advancing. So be sure to give the speaker your full attention.

When you're in the dojang, you can't just come and go as you please. This means that you must ask permission to leave early. If you're not feeling well, if you have an appointment, or if you need to leave before the end of class for any other reason, you must talk to your sabumnim first. This is so that he knows exactly where you are, and it also shows that you are a responsible person.

Finally, the most important rule. You'll hear this a lot—both in this book and from your instructor—but it can't be stressed enough: Never practice your kicks, punches, or other moves on your friends, or on other students who aren't prepared or aren't as advanced as you are. Your sabumnim will pair you with a partner who is appropriate for you, and you should respect your sabumnim's choice, even if you'd rather practice with one of your friends. If you are caught using your taekwondo moves outside of class in a way that is not appropriate, you could face very severe penalties, which might include being banned from the dojang. You should always keep in mind that taekwondo students try to live with honor and respect, and they never use their moves unless they have no other choice.

HOW TO ACT TOWARD THE TEACHER

Your taekwondo teacher, or sabumnim, is someone to whom you should show the utmost respect. This means that you should bow to him, pay close attention to what he says and does, never interrupt him when he's speaking, and address him as "mister" or "master" (for example, "Mr. Smith" or "Master Smith"). While you should feel comfortable asking your sabumnim questions, you should try to approach him only when it's really important. If you have a question, ask the other students—including the most senior student—before asking your sabumnim. This is also a way of showing respect to your

Training Tip

You should never ask your sabumnim to teach you new moves–he will instruct you at his own pace, and when he feels you are ready.

sabumnim; by only going to him with the most difficult or important questions, you're showing him that you understand that he is busy and that he should only be consulted on important issues.

HOW TO ACT TOWARD OTHER STUDENTS

When you are just beginning taekwondo, the students with more experience will look out for you and help you practice and perfect your techniques. You should show these students great respect, but you should also consider them as older brothers or sisters—people who want you to do well and will be there to help you, but who will also challenge you and expect you to work hard.

Once you have been at the dojang for a while, new students will join, and suddenly you will be the one showing others how to do things! You should take your role as a leader seriously; help these students learn the proper etiquette inside the dojang, and assist them when they are struggling with the stances, kicks, blocks, and punches that you once struggled with.

All students who practice taekwondo are part of a special family. You must treat the students around you like brothers and sisters. This also means that you are responsible for one another's actions. When one student in the class is not behaving properly, all of the students feel bad and are punished by doing at least ten push-ups. And if one does something especially well, such as winning a tournament or receiving an A on a test at school, everyone feels proud. Therefore, you should always be on your best behavior in the dojang, and you should try to help others be on their best behavior, too.

four
THE CLASS

Now that you've found the right dojang and have signed up for class, here's what you can expect during the first days of training and beyond.

BEFORE CLASS

You will probably want to show up to your class a few minutes early, if possible. This will give you time to warm up and prepare for your lesson. However, this is not the proper time or place to catch up with friends—save that for after class, once you've left the dojang. While inside the dojang, your mind should be focused on taekwondo.

You should always try your best to be on time for class and give your sabumnim warning if you know you must be late. If you arrive after class has already begun, try to be as quiet and respectful as possible. This means that you shouldn't interrupt your sabumnim, even if it's to apologize for being late. The proper time to say you're sorry is after class, once your sabumnim has a few free minutes. However, you should always bow upon first entering the dojang—even if you're late.

Bowing

Bowing (*kyung nay* in Korean) is one way taekwondo students show respect. Whenever you come to your taekwondo school you must bow to your master instructor, to any black belts, and to all of your fellow students. When you do this, they will bow back, showing that they respect you, too.

To bow correctly, you have to put your feet together and stand at attention like a soldier. Then, you should bow slowly and as low as you can. Do not look at the person you are bowing to—this means that you don't trust him and have to keep an eye on him. By not looking at the person you bow

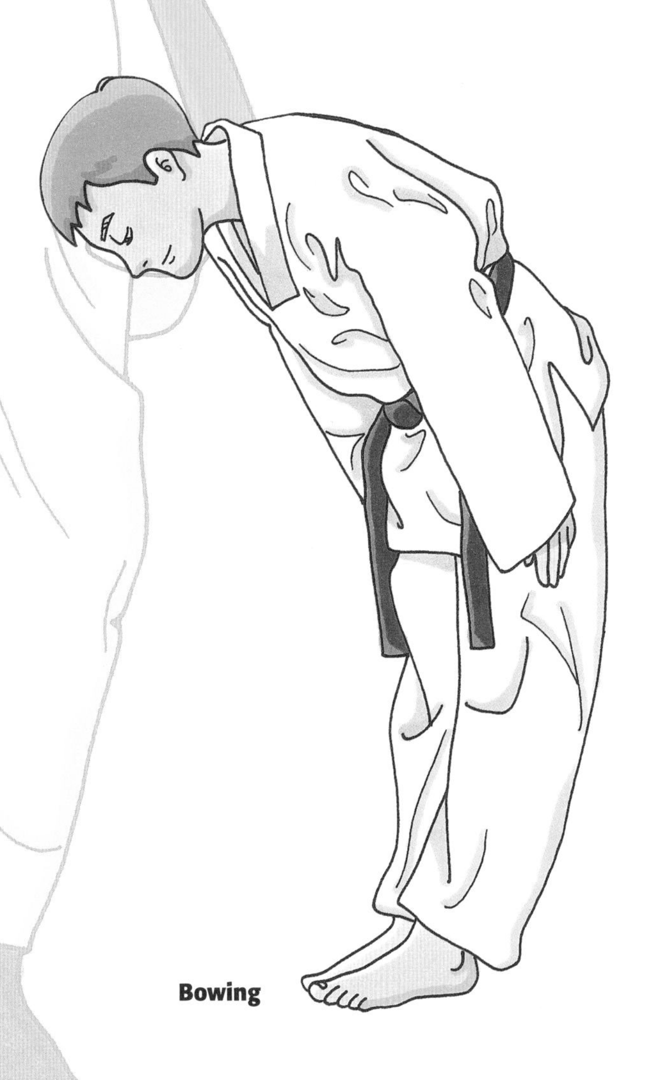

Bowing

Meditate

Meditation

Meditating is a time to focus your thoughts and mentally prepare yourself for practice. Some people like to picture their favorite places in nature–like a forest, mountain, or the ocean–when they meditate. Think of what makes you calm and happy.

to, you are showing him respect, as well as trust.

After you bow to your instructor and to your fellow students, you also bow to the Korean and your national flags. This is to show that you respect the role that both of these countries play in your life. You respect Korea because it is the home of taekwondo, and you respect the country you live in. There may also be a picture of a famous grandmaster at your dojang—if there is, you will also bow to the picture to show respect for the grandmaster.

When class is about to begin, the sabumnim will clap loudly and say "*chul sa.*" This means stop whatever you are doing and quickly, but calmly, get in line. Students will line up in order of rank—the most advanced student will stand at the front of the class, while the beginners will stand at the back of the class. The highest-ranking student will give some commands in Korean, starting with *doe rha* and *kyung yet*, which mean to turn and bow to the flags, and turn and bow to the instructor. It's okay if you don't understand the words—just do what you see everyone else doing. Next, the student will say "*an jo!*" This means sit down. Then, he will say "*cham sun*," which means meditate. You should close your eyes and try to calm your thoughts. When your sabumnim claps, you should open your eyes again. Finally, your sabumnim will say "*e la sutt*," which means stand up.

DURING CLASS

The instructor will walk everyone through the warm-up exercises, which will include some stretching. Then, the class will begin. If this is your first class, you may be told to walk around and observe the other students while they practice their kicks, punches, blocks, and forms. Or you may be asked to sit out of the way while the more advanced students practice combinations. Try not to get impatient; before you know it, you'll be learning these exact same moves—and you'll have a head start if you watch carefully and learn from others.

Blocking Practice

Blocks are a very important part of the taekwondo defense. During a typical class, your instructor will call out a block—such as a low block, outer block, or rising block—and the class will stand in rows and practice this block. There should be plenty of room between each person so that no one will accidentally get hit, and the rows should be straight and neat. Again, the most advanced students will be at the front of the class, and the beginners will be at the back. The rows move forward, practicing the blocks, until the front row reaches the wall. Then, everyone will turn around and practice the blocks going the other way.

Kicking Practice

Since the essence of taekwondo is its kicks, a lot of time will be spent working out your legs. Usually, your sabumnim will start the kicking part of class by having everyone practice the basic kicks, which include the front kick, side kick, and roundhouse kick. All students, from beginners to advanced students, will practice these same kicks. Don't be discouraged if the advanced students are able to kick much higher, straighter, or faster than you; remember, they started out just like you're starting out, and with a lot of practice you'll be able to kick like that, too!

Taekwondo Class

Each taekwondo class is made up of twelve basic parts, or elements. Some days your class might spend more time on a certain element, some days less. But you will work on each of these twelve elements throughout your time at the dojang.

1. Bowing
2. Warming up
3. Blocking practice
4. Kicking practice
5. Punching practice
6. Forms practice
7. Self-defense training
8. One-step sparring
9. Three-step sparring
10. Sparring
11. Board-breaking practice
12. Meditation

Poomse (Forms) Practice

Poomse—"forms" in Korean—are important parts of offensive and defensive taekwondo moves. With poomse, students are able to combine the various kicks, blocks, and punches that they learn.

There are two different ways to teach poomse in class. One way is for everyone to practice poomse together, starting with the most basic. Then, as the poomse become more advanced, the students who don't know them will sit down and watch the advanced students practice.

The other way is for your sabumnim to call on individual students and have them demonstrate the poomse they are working on.

Whenever you advance in taekwondo and get a new belt color, you learn a new poomse that you must practice and master.

Self-Defense Training

Self-defense is a very important part of all martial arts, so a portion of your class time will involve learning specific defensive techniques. Students will usually pair off, and one student will play the offensive role—that means he or she is the one attacking—while the other student will play the defensive role—that means he or she avoids or breaks the attack. Once again, you may just have to watch at first, since you won't yet know the defensive moves. But soon you'll learn how to block a strike, how to break a hold, and how to evade an attack.

Sparring

Sparring Practice

You probably won't practice sparring for some time. Sparring is basically practicing different kicks, punches, blocks, and poomse. Some of the more advanced students might demonstrate their skill in these areas by practicing no-contact sparring. This means that while they perform punches and kicks, they don't actually touch their opponent—or if they do touch their opponent, it is only very lightly. No-contact sparring is a good way to practice your moves and judge how an opponent will react, without worrying about hurting someone or getting hurt. However, you can only practice sparring if your sabumnim gives you permission—he will tell you when he feels you are ready. Be patient, and in the meantime watch the advanced students sparring, and try to learn from them.

Board-Breaking Practice

Board breaking is a great way for students to demonstrate how much power is behind their kicks and punches. You won't be breaking boards as a white belt, but by watching the more advanced students practice board breaking you should be able to observe how much power you'll gain during the course of your training.

END OF CLASS

The class ends like it began—by lining up in order of rank, bowing to the flags and bowing to the instructor. However, this time, when you bow to your sabumnim, you will also say, "*Gamsa hamnida*," which means "Thank you for teaching us." Your instructor will say, "*Chun mun a yoe*," which means "You're welcome."

You will also meditate again at the end of class. This may be a bit harder to do now that your adrenaline is pumping, but it's very important to calm your body and focus your mind before leaving class. Close your eyes and take slow, deep breaths. Now you are ready for life outside the dojang.

If this was your first class, you may get home and feel like you've already forgotten everything you just learned. Don't worry! The more you practice, the better you'll remember. Also, you may wake up the next morning feeling very sore. This is so because your body needs time to adjust to the new moves. Make sure you take your time stretching and warming up before and after each practice. Before you know it, you'll be performing kicks, punches, and blocks with ease!

Words to Know

Chul sa: Line up

Doe rha: Turn toward (the flag or your instructor)

Kyung yet: Bow

An jo: Sit down

Myung sang: Meditate

E la sutt: Stand up

Gamsa hamnida: "Thank you for teaching us."

Chun mun a yoe: "You're welcome."

Safety

At first, it may seem like things inside the dojang are pretty strict: You have to wear a uniform; you have to bow and be respectful to your sabumnim; and you can't wrestle around or joke with your friends. But you'll quickly realize that all of these rules are for the best; without them, people could very easily get hurt.

Here are some other safety tips to keep in mind when practicing taekwondo.

- *Keep your nails short*: This may sound silly, but it can be really dangerous to have long nails or ragged nails—you could cut or scratch yourself or other students while practicing. Also, you might not be able to make a fist properly. So be sure to keep your nails trimmed neatly.

- *Remove all jewelry*: Before practicing, take off your watch, rings, or other jewelry that you have on, as they could get caught in someone's hair or uniform, or even cut someone. If you have any jewelry that can't be taken off—such as earrings that need to be kept in—then be sure to cover these items with athletic tape. You may feel and look a bit silly, but it's better than hurting yourself, or someone else.

- *Take your time and be precise*: Once you've been to class a few times, you'll probably be one of the students practicing your techniques. An easy way to hurt yourself, or someone else, is to practice your kicks and punches too fast, or sloppily. You should be slow and precise in whatever you do, and you should never try to show off—you won't learn much that way, and you could even wind up hurting yourself. Try not to watch other students while you practice, unless you're hoping to learn from them. Remember, the class is not a competition, and it's important for you to have a solid foundation if you want to advance.

WHAT'S NEXT?

It's important for you to keep in mind that taekwondo is not a sport in the same way that football, baseball, and soccer are sports. Martial arts are ways of life—this means that while you learn kicks and punches, you also learn how to treat others with respect, how to be humble (which means you don't show off), and how to work hard. All of these things take a lot of time to learn, and you'll have to practice for years before you know the moves—and the way of life—of a black belt. Be patient, and treat each class as an important step along the way.

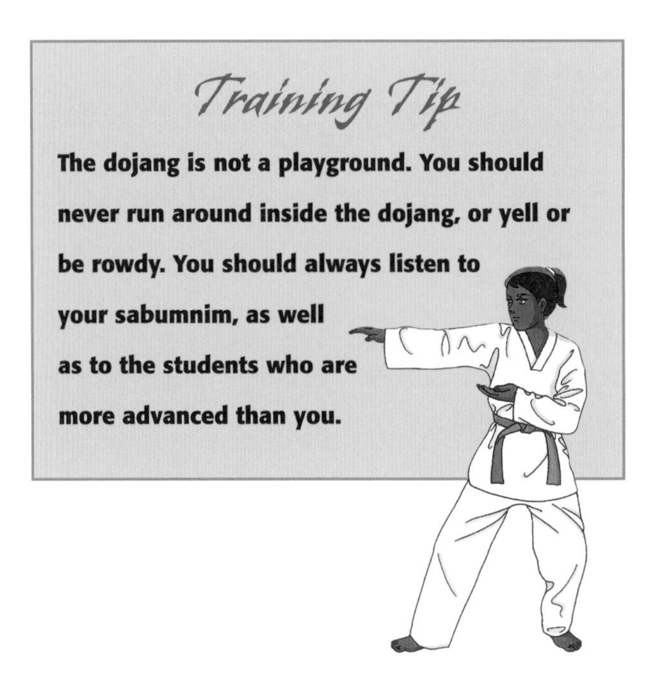

five

WARMING UP AND STRETCHING

You're probably anxious to learn more about the kicks, punches, and blocks of taekwondo. But these moves require flexibility (loose muscles). Stretching will loosen up your muscles and give you flexibility. Once you're flexible, you'll be able to kick high, punch hard, and block quickly.

Forward stretch

WARMING UP

Before you stretch, you should first warm up. You can do lots of things to warm up, such as jumping jacks or running in place. There are also a few "mini-stretches" that you can do, which don't work your muscles as much as regular stretches. Here are a few warm-ups you can try.

FORWARD MINI-STRETCH

Stand with your legs spread. If you feel pain or if your legs start to shake, this means that you're spreading your legs too far. If that happens, bring them closer together. Now, keep your legs spread and bend forward at the waist, placing your hands on the ground in front of you. If you can't stretch that far yet, don't worry—just lean forward as far as you can without hurting yourself. With enough practice, you'll soon be flexible enough to touch the ground.

Don't forget to warm up! If you don't prepare your body for the stretching, kicking, and punching you're about to do, you could seriously hurt yourself.

SIDE AND BACK MINI-STRETCH

From the forward mini-stretch, straighten up and put your left hand on your hip. Raise your right hand over your head and lean side-ways to the left, bending at your waist. Be sure to stretch out your right arm—this will work the muscles in your side and your lower back.

Side and back stretch

Hold this stretch for a minute. Stand up straight again and then switch sides, placing your right hand at your waist and stretching your left hand across your head while you bend toward the right. Do this stretch about three times on each side, holding the stretch for a minute every time.

WINDMILLS

This warm-up is called Windmills because when you do it, you make a circular movement, and you look like a windmill. Stand with your feet slightly apart and with your arms straight down at your sides. Raise your right arm out in front of you, then up over your head and back behind you so that you make a full circle. Next, do the same thing with your left arm. Always keep your arms straight when doing windmills and be sure to do both sides, one after the other. Do this about twenty times—but don't go too fast. You want to loosen up your body, not pull your muscles! After doing these warm-ups, you'll be ready to stretch.

Windmills 1

Windmills 2

STRETCHING

Now that your blood is pumping quicker and your muscles are awake, you can begin stretching. This is an essential part of your taekwondo practice—taekwondo features some impressive kicks, and you can't do these kicks unless you're very flexible. Stretching thoroughly and slowly before each practice is the only way to become flexible.

Lunge stretch

LUNGE STRETCH

Start by spreading your legs about twice as wide as your shoulders, with one leg out in front of you and the other leg behind you. Your front leg should be bent at the knee, and your back leg should be straight and low to the ground. Try to keep the heel of your back leg flat on the floor. Next, lean forward on the bent knee and get even lower to the ground.

If your legs shake or hurt a lot when stretching, this means that you're trying to do too much all at once. Take your time and relax.

You should feel the stretch along the inside of your back leg. Try to press the knee of your back leg to the ground—but be sure not to lift your heel! Hold this stretch for about thirty seconds and then switch sides. Do this stretch at least three times on each side.

HURDLER'S STRETCH

You'll need to sit down for this stretch. Bend your right leg back and keep your left leg straight with your toes pointed up. If this hurts a lot, you can bring your bent knee closer to your straight leg. This will take away the pain. When you find a spot you're pretty comfortable in, reach forward to your straight leg. Stay there for a while, then reach to the space between your bent leg and your straight leg. After that, bring your head as close to your knee as you can. Stay there a while, then do the same thing on the opposite side. This is called the hurdler's stretch. It was given this name because when you do it, you'll look like someone who's jumping over a hurdle.

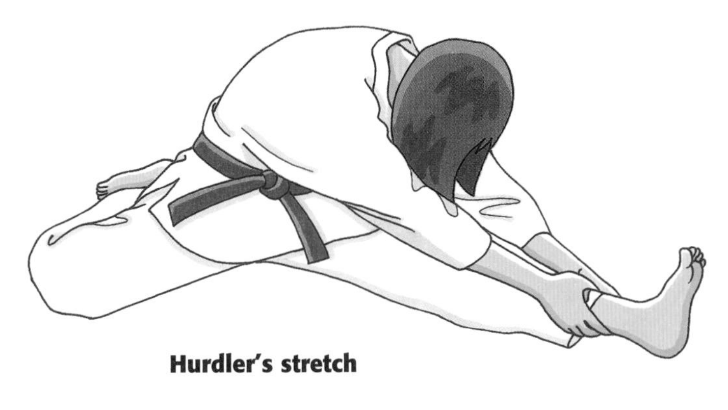

Hurdler's stretch

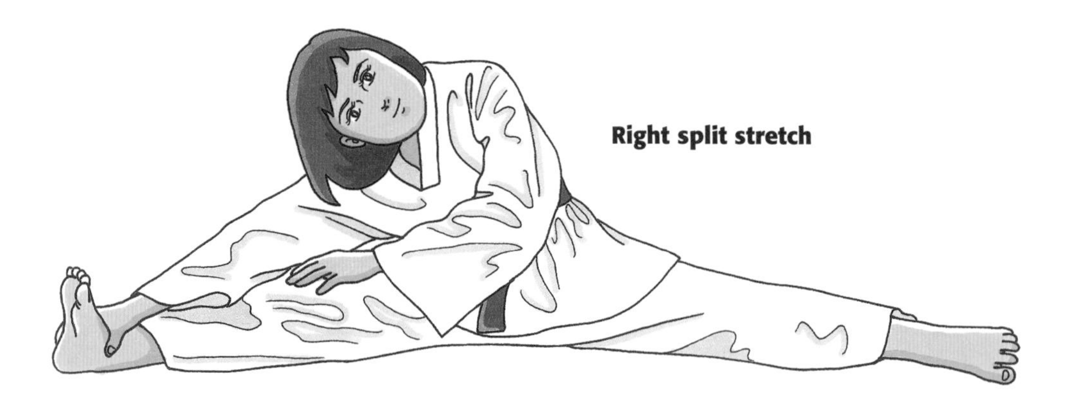
Right split stretch

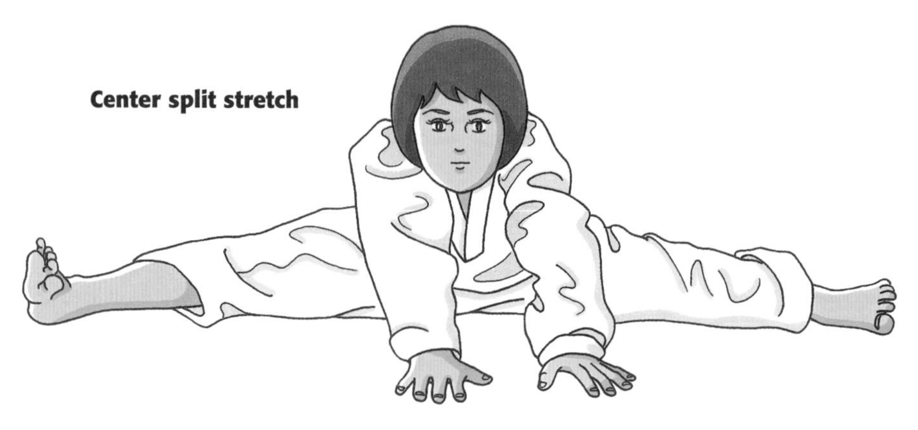
Center split stretch

SPLIT STRETCH

For the split stretch, point both feet straight in front of you. Keep your legs together and your toes pointed up as you reach forward. Then, spread your legs as far as they will go. Reach toward each leg and to the middle for about twenty seconds each.

BUTTERFLY STRETCH

For the last stretch, bring the heels of your feet together and pull them in. Now shake your legs a little. This is called the butterfly stretch because your legs will make a shape like a butterfly.

Now that you've warmed up and stretched, you're ready to start kicking.

Butterfly stretch

If you take your time and do your stretches right, they will make you more flexible. This means that you will be able to kick higher, faster, and more powerfully.

six

PRACTICING TAEKWONDO

As you know, it is very important that you understand the basics of taekwondo before moving to more advanced techniques. If you understand the basics well, you will have a strong foundation upon which you can build. Think of a tall building. If it has a strong foundation, it will always stand tall. If its foundation is weak, it could crumble because it doesn't have support at its bottom. It's the same thing in taekwondo. Without strength in the basics, it is impossible to improve. The techniques we are about to discuss are some of the basics you'll need. You should practice them as much as possible at the dojang as well as at home.

You will have to learn basic stances and blocks before you can practice the punches and kicks of taekwondo. Some of the stances you'll need are the horseback-riding stance (*juchoom sogi*), forward stance (*ahp-gubi*), back stance (*dwi-gibi sogi*), and walking stance (*ahp sogi*). The blocks you'll need include the low block (*ahre maggi*), inner block (*momtong ahn maggi*), outer block (*momtong bakat maggi*), and rising block (*eolgul maggi*). Let's go over them one by one and then get into some punching and kicking.

STANCES

Imagine throwing a hard punch at a heavy bag while leaning back. You'd probably fall down. Now imagine leaning into your punch with all your weight—this time it's the bag that goes flying! How you stand is very important in taekwondo. It can decide whether it's you or the other guy who's going to fall down.

But before moving on to stances that you'll use in practice, there are two very basic stances you must know: the attention stance (*charyot sogi*) and the ready stance (*jumbi sogi*).

Words to Know

Stances (Sogi)

Charyot sogi: Attention stance

Jumbi sogi: Ready stance

Ahp-gubi sogi: Forward stance

Dwi-gibi sogi: Back stance

Ahp sogi: Walking stance

Kyroogi ja-say: Fighting stance

Juchoom sogi: Horseback-riding stance

Whenever you learn a stance, block, or strike in taekwondo, you must know its name in both English and Korean. If it's hard to remember, try saying it whenever you do it.

ATTENTION STANCE (CHARYOT SOGI)

One of the very first things you will learn when you come to your taekwondo school is to stand at attention. The stance used for this is called charyot sogi, which means attention stance. All you have to do is place your feet together, put your hands directly at your sides, and look straight ahead. It is important that you pay careful attention to what your sabumnim is saying when you are in this stance, and if you can stay in it for a long time, this means that you are concentrating well.

Attention stance

READY STANCE (JUMBI SOGI)

Usually, the first thing you will do from you attention stance (charyot sogi) is move into a ready stance. In Korean, the ready stance is called jumbi sogi. Remember, you must first be in an attention stance before you can go into a ready stance. To do it, simply make your hands into fists and step sideways with your left leg so that your legs are shoulders'-width apart.

Ready stance

FORWARD STANCE (AHP-GUBI SOGI)

Imagine being able to take all of your energy and put it behind a single punch. The force would be incredible! When you practice your forward stance, called ahp-gubi sogi in Korean, you'll be taking your first step in learning how to punch with this kind of power. This is so because the way you stand has a lot to do with how hard you can punch or kick.

Forward stance

To practice the forward stance, start out by standing with your feet shoulders'-width apart. Now step forward with your left leg to a distance that is twice as wide as your shoulders. Bend your forward leg and keep the heels of both feet on the ground. Sometimes, when students are first learning the forward stance, they will lift the heel of their back foot. This is wrong—be sure to keep both feet planted firmly on the ground. Most of your weight should be on the foot that is forward (in this example, that would be your left foot). You should be "full-bodied" whenever you do a forward stance, meaning that the upper part of your body should be facing completely forward, not sideways. To do this, you must keep your back straight at all times.

BACK STANCE (DWI-GIBI SOGI)

If you're serious about taekwondo, then you'll have to be serious about your back stance (dwi-gibi sogi). It's one of the most important stances you'll learn, and all taekwondo students must be able to do it well. To practice, start with your feet together, facing front. Now turn your right foot so that it is pointing to the wall on your right. Your feet are now making a 90-degree angle. Now step back with your right leg. You should step back the distance of a shoulders'-width and a half.

This is called a back stance because almost all of your weight is on your back leg. If you can lift up your front foot pretty easily when doing the back stance, then you're doing it well. If you first have to lean

Back stance

back a little to do this, you'll have to lean back more from the start. When you do a back stance, your rear foot should be in line with your front foot. You should, for instance, be able to do a back stance on a tightrope. Your upper body should be at a 45-degree angle—that just means it should be partially turned, instead of facing straight forward.

WALKING STANCE (AHP SOGI)

Do you want to become great at taekwondo? If so, the first thing you'll need is the walking stance, or ahp sogi. Once you learn the walking stance, you'll have a good idea about how to make a fighting stance. The walking stance is one of the most important stances in taekwondo because it is used so much during fighting. It is also one of the easiest stances to learn. Simply face forward with your legs shoulders'-width apart. Now just take a regular step forward. That's it! A walking stance is easy and comfortable. This will become

Walking stance

important as you learn fighting because you'll want to be able to move in any direction at any time. If you are comfortable in your stance, you'll be able to do this. If not, then you'll have to shift your weight before you move. This could waste precious seconds that you might need to do a kick.

FIGHTING STANCE (KYROOGI JA-SAY)

From the walking stance, all you'll have to do to be in a fighting stance (kyroogi ja-say) is put your hands up. Your front hand should be at about eye height and your rear hand a little lower.

Fighting stance

When in a fighting stance, you should always be bouncing a little on the balls of your feet. In ancient times, taekwondo practitioners would sit back in a long, wide stance. But in more modern days, the masters of taekwondo discovered that you can kick much more easily if you are in a comfortable stance, standing upright and ready for anything.

HORSEBACK-RIDING STANCE (JUCHOOM SOGI)

One of the very first stances you will learn is the horseback-riding stance. In Korean its name is juchoom sogi. You'll need this stance before you can learn any blocks, since

Horseback-riding stance

at first most blocks are done from this stance. It is called the horseback-riding stance because when you do it, your legs and feet are in a position similar to that of a person riding a horse. If you have ever ridden a horse, you may have noticed that your toes point in a little and that your knees point out. You keep your back straight and look ahead. You must do all of these things when in your horseback-riding stance.

To begin practicing the horseback-riding stance, stand with your feet together. Now spread them apart about two times as wide as your shoulders. Next, point your toes in a little, and bend your knees so that they are almost as far out as your toes. You must keep your back upright. Remember to look straight ahead. As you start to practice techniques from this stance, try not to wobble. It is important that you stay in a good stance as you block or punch.

BLOCKS

LOW BLOCK (AHRE MAGGI)

The first block you will learn from the horseback-riding stance is the low block—in Korean, that's ahre maggi. If someone were to try to kick you, a low block would be a great way to defend yourself. To practice, stay in a good horseback-riding stance (juchoom sogi) and make fists with both hands. Bring your left fist to your right ear and point your right fist straight down. Now snap your left hand down really fast as you bring your right hand to your waist. That's all there is to it! Be sure to practice on both sides, and remember to yell out the block's name. So, as you do a low block, you should always shout, "low block!" or "ahre maggi!"

It is important that the hand that is not blocking be brought back to the spot on your body that is just above your belt. Be sure to keep the palm of this hand pointed up. The more you practice taekwondo blocks and strikes, the more you will notice that

Low block

The low block, or ahre maggi, will help you defend against kicks.

Words to Know

Blocks (Maggi)

Ahre maggi: Low block

Momtong ahn maggi: Inner block

Momtong bakat maggi: Outer block

Eolgul maggi: Rising block

when you do any of them, you make a twisting motion with both hands. This means that if you are doing a low block with your left hand, the left hand twists as it goes down, and the right hand twists as it goes to the spot above your belt. This twisting will give your block or punch better form and more power. You should always do a block or strike as fast as possible.

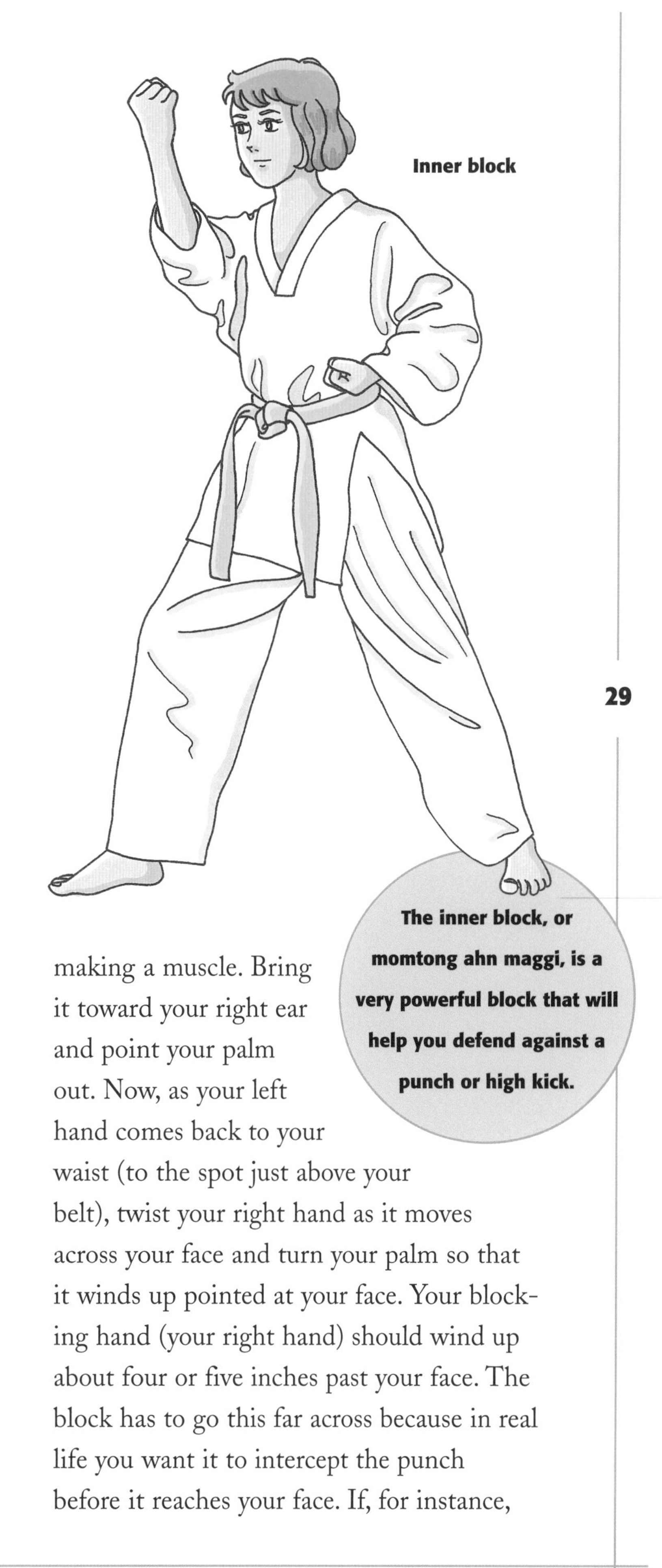

Inner block

The inner block, or momtong ahn maggi, is a very powerful block that will help you defend against a punch or high kick.

INNER BLOCK (MOMTONG AN MAGGI)

Most people who do not know taekwondo will try to punch in a circular way. This means that the punch comes around instead of straight at you. An inner block (momtong ahn maggi) is one of the best ways to defend against this kind of punch. To practice, stay in the horseback-riding stance (juchoom sogi) you used for your low block. Now, make fists with both hands and point your left hand straight out in front of you as if you have just made a punch. Lift up your right hand just as you would if you were making a muscle. Bring it toward your right ear and point your palm out. Now, as your left hand comes back to your waist (to the spot just above your belt), twist your right hand as it moves across your face and turn your palm so that it winds up pointed at your face. Your blocking hand (your right hand) should wind up about four or five inches past your face. The block has to go this far across because in real life you want it to intercept the punch before it reaches your face. If, for instance, you only blocked as far as your nose, someone could punch your cheek. So always be sure to bring your blocks past the spot the other person is trying to hit.

OUTER BLOCK (MOMTONG BAKAT MAGGI)

Another important block you'll need to know is the outer block, which in Korean is called momtong bakat maggi. Be sure you stay in the same horseback-riding stance as before. To practice, make fists and give yourself a big hug. Keep your left hand under your right. When you do an outer block, the hand that's underneath is always the blocking hand. Point the palm of your blocking hand toward the floor. Now, swing that hand (your left hand) up and across until it passes your face by about three or four inches. At the same time, bring your right hand back to the spot just above your belt. As with the other blocks you're learning, this twisting motion is very important. When you do the outer block, don't forget to yell "momtong bakat maggi!" If you need help with your pronunciation, don't be afraid to ask. Your sabumnim will be glad to help.

The outer block, or momtong bakat maggi, will help you to defend your face against all sorts of attacks.

Outer block

RISING BLOCK (EOLGUL MAGGI)

What if someone were to try to hit you from above? Your best bet is to do a rising block, or eolgul maggi. It is called a rising block because it rises upward. This block works like a charm, and it's easy to do. To practice, make fists and then put your hands in front of your face and make an X with them. Keep your left hand on the outside of the X. Remember, when you do a rising block, the hand that is blocking is always on the outside of the X. Now slide your left hand up (this is your blocking hand) and bring your right hand back to the spot that's just above your belt. Twist your blocking arm so that the meaty, muscular part of your arm is facing up, not the bone. It could hurt

Rising block

you to block with your bone, so be sure to twist your arm when you block. Remember that the hand that is not blocking also makes a twisting movement as it goes to your waist. When you get it to your waist, be sure to keep your palm pointed up. And don't forget to yell "eolgul maggi!" when you practice your rising block.

Training Tip

When you do a punch or a block in the horseback-riding stance, be sure that the hand that is not punching or blocking returns to the right spot—above your waist with the palm pointed up.

KICKS

FRONT SNAP KICK (AHP CHA-GI)

The first kick you'll need to learn is the front snap kick, called *ahp cha-gi* in Korean. Like most kicks, the best way to learn the front snap kick is in four parts. Start from your fighting stance (kyroogi ja-say) with your left side forward and your right side back. First, lift up your right knee as you

Front snap kick 1

Front snap kick 2

Be sure to practice all kicks with both your right and left legs.

bring it forward and curl your toes up. Second, snap the kick straight out as fast as you can. Third, quickly snap it back. Fourth, put it back in the exact spot it left from.

When you do the front snap kick, you have to bring your right hand forward and up a little. This is so because when you do a fighting stance, the hand that's behind is a little lower than the one in front. And since when you do the first part of the front snap kick your shoulders are facing front, you have to raise the hand that is back a little so that you can protect your face while you kick. Keep in mind that one of the best times to kick someone is while he or she is kicking. So always keep your hands up when you kick. Your front snap kick should come straight out. This is very important. As you may know, the shortest distance between two points is a straight line. So, you might want to practice in front of a mirror and make sure that your kick comes straight out. Whenever you do your front snap kick, be sure to yell out "ahp cha-gi!"

Words to Know

Kicks (Cha-gi)

Ahp cha-gi: Front snap kick

Dolryo cha-gi: Roundhouse kick

Yop cha-gi: Side kick

Neria cha-gi: Axe kick

ROUNDHOUSE KICK (DOLRYO CHA-GI)

The roundhouse kick, called dolryo cha-gi in Korean, is the most popular kick in taekwondo. Why? Because it's so fast that it's totally amazing! Also, the roundhouse kick works really well, and you can use it almost any time you want. It works when you throw it to the middle section of your opponent, such as the ribs, or to the high section, such as the head. Some of the most famous competitors in the world use the roundhouse more than any other kick. So, you should definitely practice it as much as you can.

Roundhouse kick 1

Again, the best way to learn this kick is to break it into four simple parts. Start from your fighting stance and put your right side back. First, lift your right leg (that's the one in the back) as you turn on the ball of your left (forward) foot. While doing this, you'll have to bring your right hand up. Since you switch sides as you kick, you need to use your rear hand to protect your head. Otherwise, your head will be open, and someone can hit it. Your knee should be pointed a little past your target. Second, snap the kick out and hit with your instep (that's the side part of your foot—so don't curl your toes back as you do when you perform the front snap kick).

Roundhouse kick 2

Third, bring the leg back to the way it was in the first part. Fourth, put it down in the spot it left from. When you start to practice sparring, you'll find that it's better to land forward instead of bringing your leg back to the spot you started from. But in the meantime, this is the best way to practice.

When your leg is straight, make sure that it is lined up with your back. To help you understand this, imagine your roundhouse kick to be straight out. Now, imagine someone placing a yardstick that goes from your side down your leg. If you are doing the kick right, you'll see no space between your leg, your side, and the yardstick. If you're doing it wrong by leaning forward, you will see space, and the more you see, the more incorrect your kick is.

Even though this is a great kick, you'll have to practice it many times before you get it right. When you improve, your kick will have better "form." If your sabumnim says your kick has good form, that means you are doing the motion of the kick right. Every time you do a kick, you are taking a step in improving your form. This is so because it takes a lot of repetition (doing something over and over again) to make your form better. To get a great roundhouse kick, you'll have to do lots of repetitions. But if you listen well to your sabumnim and practice at home, you'll find yourself getting better every day!

SIDE KICK (YOP CHA-GI)

One of the toughest kicks to learn is the side kick, or yop cha-gi in Korean. One reason is that so many people confuse it with the roundhouse kick. In fact, the side kick is totally different from the roundhouse kick, and it should always be clear to your sabumnim which kick you're doing. To practice a side kick, start once again from your fighting stance (kyroogi ja-say) with your right side back. As usual, there are four parts: First, lift your right knee up and all the way around so that it touches (or almost touches) the left side of your chest. As you do this, pivot on your left foot, and switch your hands so that the hand that was behind

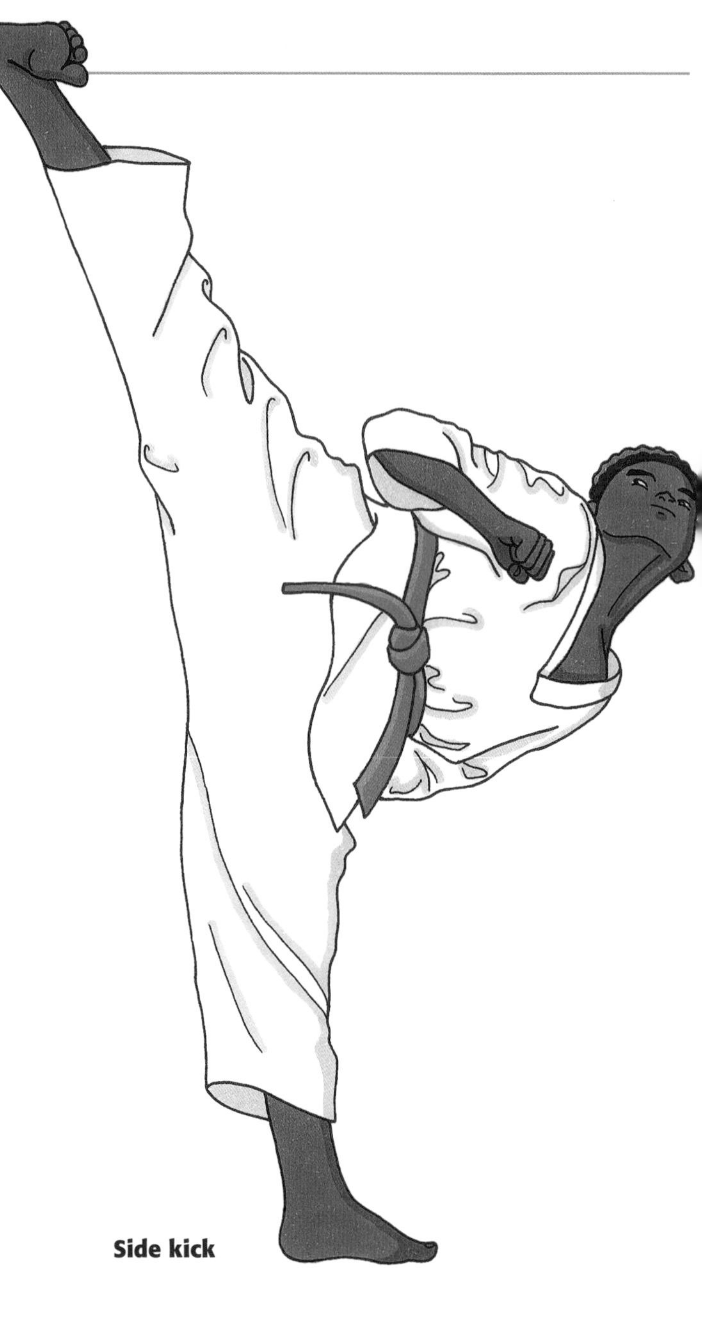

Side kick

(your right hand) is now protecting your head. And remember, the best time to kick someone is when he or she is kicking. So, switch your hands when you throw a side kick and protect your head. Otherwise, you could run into big trouble.

Second, extend your leg straight out and push out your heel. This is the part of your foot you hit with when you do a side kick. You'll need to try extra hard to make sure that your heel is sticking out. Your leg should form a straight line with the side of your body. That means do not bend your upper body. A lot of beginners make that mistake. One good way to avoid doing this is to practice your kick in the mirror. And, as always, you should feel free to demonstrate a kick for your sabumnim, so he may give you ideas on how to improve it.

AXE KICK (NERIA CHA-GI)

The axe kick (neria cha-gi) is one of the most exciting kicks in taekwondo. Someone who has a good axe kick, such as a black belt, can swing his leg straight up so it's pointing directly at the sky. He can then land the heel of his leg on his opponent's face or chest as it comes down. A good axe kicker can do this so fast that his opponent never knows what hit him! The motion looks like that of an axe, because the kick swings up and then straight down. Of course, this is not the sort of thing you'll want to practice on your friends. As with all kicks, you must only practice it when you are being supervised (watched) by an adult. You can only use your kicks in competition where everyone is wearing protective gear, or if you are attacked and face serious danger. To practice the axe kick, start off in your fighting stance (kyroogi ja-say) with your right leg back. As you'll remember, we did all the other kicks in four parts. The axe kick, however, is a little different—it's not

Axe kick

good to think of it as having separate parts. Instead, try to think of it as one fluid motion. This will help you do it quickly and neatly. To practice, swing your rear leg up as high as you can, keeping it slightly bent as you do this. As the leg comes down, you should snap it. You'll get amazing power from the combination of snap and swing. You should land the kick with your heel. The axe kick is almost always thrown to the face, although you can occasionally throw it to the chest.

At first, you probably won't be able to perform a lot of these kicks—especially the axe kick. You will need to practice a lot and become more flexible. As your flexibility improves, you will find that you are able to throw all of your kicks faster and better. This is especially true about the axe kick; to throw an axe kick right, you must not only kick to the height of your own head, but way above it. Remember, the kick winds up landing on the other person's face after it rises way up above it. It takes lots of hard work and practice to throw a good axe kick. You will also need to learn a little about timing to make this kick work. Timing means that you can't just throw a kick any time you want; you have to throw it when the time is right. One good way to learn about timing is by practicing in sparring (fighting) class about three times a week.

Safety Tip

Kicks and punches are weapons—do not practice these moves on your friends! You or they could get seriously hurt. Also, you should never attempt to perform moves that you haven't yet been taught, even if you see other students practicing them. Remember, safety first!

OTHER MOVES

MIDDLE PUNCH (MOMTONG CHIRUGI)

The middle punch, or momtong chirugi, is the first punch you will learn in your taekwondo school. To practice it, start in your horseback-riding stance (remember, that's juchoom sogi in Korean) and make fists. Point your left fist directly in front of your body so that it winds up crossing about half of your chest. You should always make contact with your two big knuckles (the knuckles of your index and middle fingers), so make sure they are sticking out more than your smaller knuckles. Now that you have your left hand in front of you in a fist, you are ready to punch—with your right hand. Do you remember the twisting movement we discussed earlier? This is also very important for your middle punch. As your left hand comes back to the spot just above your belt at your waist, snap your right hand out. Be sure that the palm of

PALM STRIKE (BATONGSON CHIRUGI)

Unlike a punch, the palm strike (batongson chirugi) uses a flat surface—your palm—as the striking surface. This strike is particularly effective against tender areas on your opponent, such as below his nose or on his temples. To perform the palm strike, bend your fingers at the second knuckles so that your fingertips rest against the top of your palm. Notice how the muscles in your hand are now tight—this creates a very powerful striking weapon. Next, bring your palm to your shoulder and snap your arm forward.

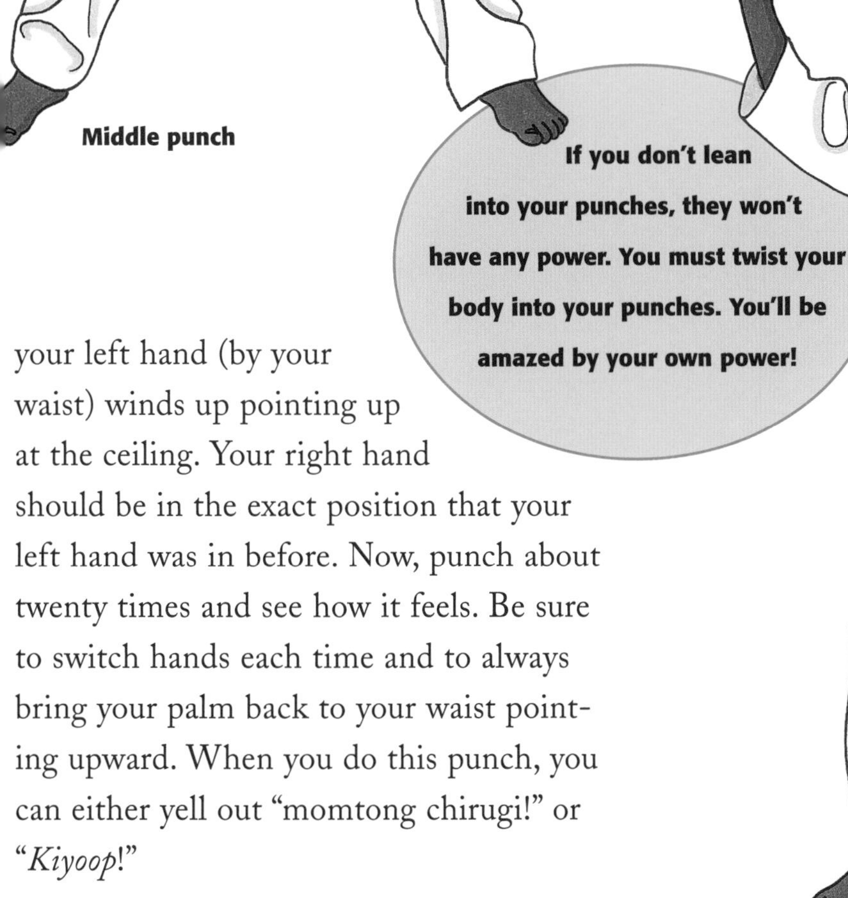

Middle punch

If you don't lean into your punches, they won't have any power. You must twist your body into your punches. You'll be amazed by your own power!

your left hand (by your waist) winds up pointing up at the ceiling. Your right hand should be in the exact position that your left hand was in before. Now, punch about twenty times and see how it feels. Be sure to switch hands each time and to always bring your palm back to your waist pointing upward. When you do this punch, you can either yell out "momtong chirugi!" or "*Kiyoop*!"

Palm strike

KNIFE HAND (SOONAL)

For the knife hand (soonal), your fingers are extended so that the muscles and tendons in your hand and wrist are tight. The part of the hand you will strike with is the base of your hand, which is the fleshy area between your wrist and the base of your pinkie finger. Like the palm strike, the knife hand is most effective against tender parts of an opponent, such as the front of his neck or the sides of his ribs. To strike with the knife hand, extend your arm toward your opponent, but be sure to keep your elbow slightly bent. If you straighten your arm completely, your knife hand strike will not be as precise, which means your aim might be off.

In addition to keeping your elbow slightly bent, be sure to maintain the tension in your hand. Many beginners make the mistake of relaxing their knife hand either just before they strike or right as the strike is delivered. This is very dangerous—you could even break the bones in your hand if you're not careful. Therefore, it is very important that you take your time when practicing your moves and be precise.

Knife hand

ELBOW STRIKE (PAL KUP)

The elbow strike (pal kup) is very effective in close-contact fighting. To perform this strike, stand with your feet shoulders'-width apart, and bend your elbow so that the bone sticks out in front of you. You will use this bone to strike with. Bring your elbow up to the level of your shoulder. Next, step forward with your lead foot (usually your right foot) and twist at your waist, swinging your elbow toward your opponent. You should be able to strike your opponent in the face or neck with your elbow. For added support, you may wish to grab the wrist of your striking arm as you twist your body.

The "Kiyoop!"

A kiyoop is a very loud yell that comes from the pit of your stomach. It will give you

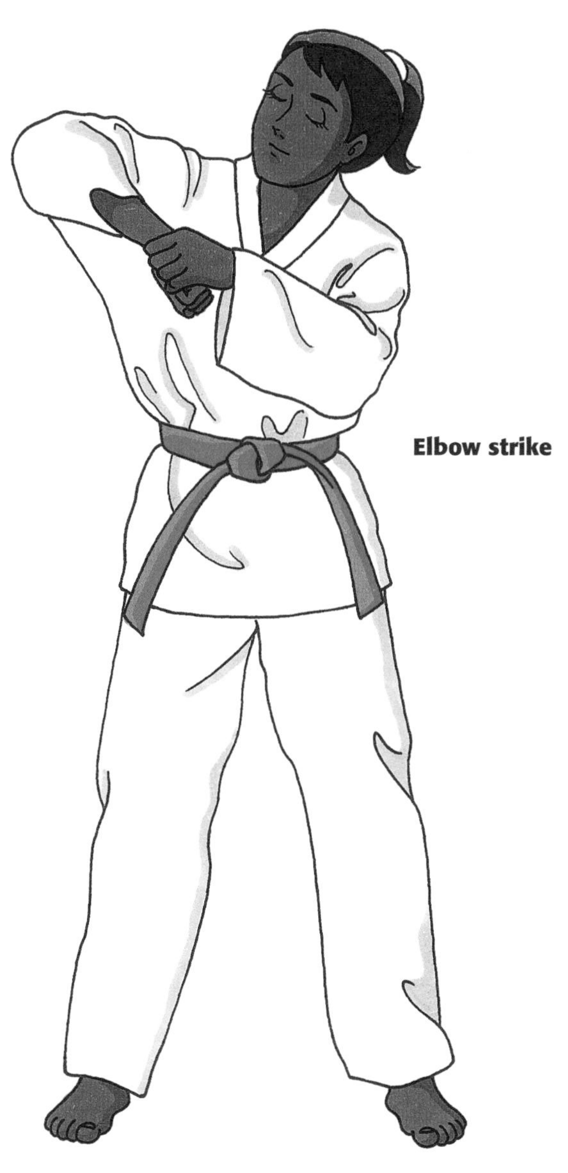

Elbow strike

more power; it will improve your confidence; and—if you do it right—it will scare your opponent. If you throw a technique without a kiyoop or with a weak kiyoop, this means that you probably do not have a lot of confidence in your taekwondo skill. But if you scream out "kiyoop!" as loudly as you can, you'll feel great, and you'll probably scare your opponent so much that he'll freeze up. Did you ever see a television show where a big bird flies down from the sky and eats a mouse? If so, you may have noticed that the bird screams very loudly right before it gets to the mouse. This makes the mouse so scared that it doesn't move at all, and the bird eats it up. It's the same thing with people. If you scream really loudly and have confidence in your techniques, the other guy will be so scared he'll just stand still. Then, it will be much easier for you to hit him. As we've discussed many times, taekwondo people never use their fighting skills unless it is absolutely necessary. But, when you do use them, do so with confidence and kiyoop as loudly as you can!

POOMSE (FORMS)

As we mentioned earlier, poomse are forms in which you combine some of the moves that you have learned. Did you ever see a gymnast do a floor routine? If so, you may have noticed that the gymnast not only memorized a set of movements, but did them well—as if she had done them thousands of times. To do poomse, you will need to know your stances, blocks, and strikes well enough to use them in combinations. When you do any taekwondo technique, you

> *Taekwondo Tip*
>
> **Poomse practice is a time when your mind and body work together. Your mind has to remember all of the kicks, punches, blocks, and stances in a set order, and your body must do them all the way you want.**

have to use your mind and your body. This is especially true when doing poomse because you have to memorize the whole form, and a form can have as many as thirty-six movements! And not only do you have to memorize the form, you must do it as closely to perfect as possible!

The first poomse you will learn is called the H form. It is called the H form because when you do it, you are moving in the same directions you need to make the letter H. As you practice the H form, you may find it helpful to remember what part of the H you are on. It takes lots of concentration to do a form right, especially when you are doing it for the first time.

Can anyone do a poomse perfectly? The answer is no. You can always punch a little faster, kick a little higher, and move a little more smoothly. A black belt in taekwondo can do his forms better than people with lower belts, but even a master of taekwondo will tell you that his form is not perfect. This is because everyone has his or her own idea of what a perfect form looks like. And just when you find you can do it in a way you thought was perfect, your idea of what a perfect form is changes. Why? Because as you get better you will set higher goals for yourself. Once you reach a goal in taekwondo, you will find that you have already set a new, higher one. That is just one of the many joys of this ancient Korean art: the more you learn, the more you want to know, and the better you'll get. You can get better in taekwondo your whole life! You don't have to be a black belt to understand this, but when you become one, you may appreciate it a little more. The first step is simply getting started.

seven

ADVANCING IN TAEKWONDO

There are two different ways to advance in taekwondo: belt tests and competitions. In belt tests, you must show that you have mastered all of the moves and poomse for your belt color and are ready to advance. In competitions, you must use your kicks, punches, blocks, and poomse, and your head, to compete against other students. Advancing is a great way for you to prove to your sabumnim, and yourself, that you're ready to learn even more!

TESTING FOR BELT PROMOTION

During belt tests, a lot of people watch you as you show the new techniques you have learned since you got your last belt. This can be a really scary experience. Usually, your family and friends are watching, as well as all of your taekwondo classmates and your sabumnim. It is your job to stay focused, concentrate, and show your sabumnim that you deserve to move up to a higher belt. With the right attitude and a lot of hard work, you will take a belt test every three months, and you'll pass each time with flying colors!

One part of your belt test is oral. That means that you have to talk to your sabumnim during the test. He will ask you questions about taekwondo's history and philosophy. You must answer the questions correctly and also show your good attitude and respect by ending each sentence with "sir!" You will stand at attention, speak politely, and demonstrate for everyone how you have improved. It is important for you to learn to speak in front of a lot of people. In regular school, you may have to give reports to a whole class of students. And when you get older, you may have to give other talks, called "presentations," to the people you work with. So it's important that you get experience in speaking in front of lots of people now. When you're older it will then be very easy.

Training Tip

During a belt test, you must show that you can kick and punch well. But you must also show that you can speak about taekwondo's history and philosophy.

ENTERING A TOURNAMENT

As you get better in taekwondo, you may want to get experience as a competitor. Taekwondo competition is safe and fun, but you'll have to practice a lot to be ready. You'll also have to know the rules of taekwondo competition. There are three ways to compete: poomse (forms), *kyroogi* (sparring), and *kyuk pah* (board breaking).

Poomse (Forms) Tournaments

During forms competition, you do the form you know for your belt (you learn a new form whenever you get a new belt). You are judged by three judges (or *bu sim* in Korean), and

SPARRING SETUP

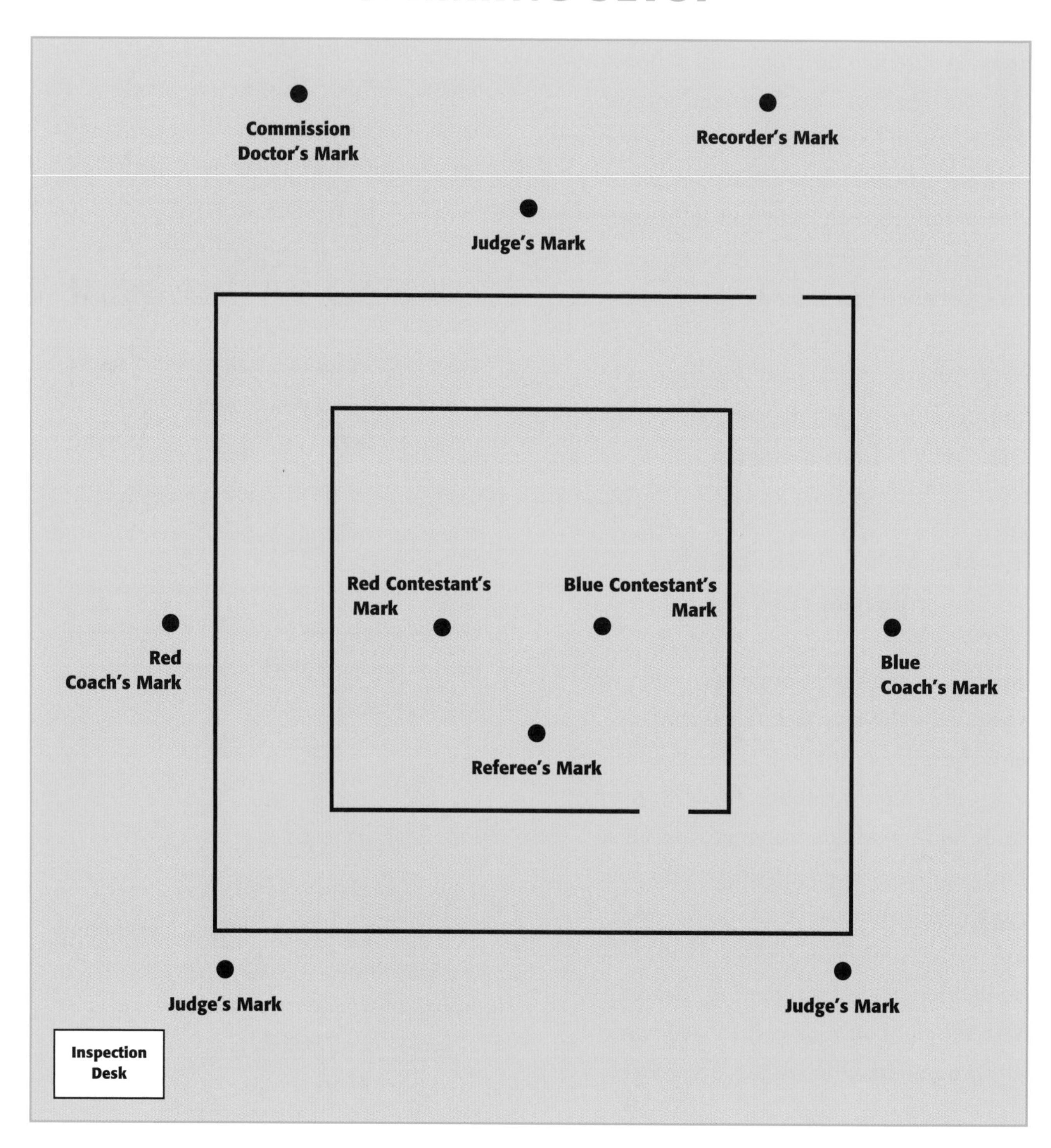

whoever does the best job and gets the highest score wins. The judges will look at many things; the way you introduce yourself, your appearance, and the way you do your form are all important. You should always go to a competition looking your best and ready to do a good job in a form you know well.

Padding

Kyroogi (Sparring) Tournaments

Many people find sparring competition (kyroogi in Korean) to be the most exciting part of a tournament.

During your match, you will see that there are four judges (bu sim) and a referee (*joo sim*). The judges each sit in a corner, but the referee stays in the ring with you throughout the match to watch out for your safety and to enforce all the rules.

The two people who are going to spar each wear a different color chest protector. One wears red, *hong* in Korean, and must stand to the left of the referee. The other wears blue, *chung* in Korean, and stands to the right of the referee. Before you begin sparring, you bow to your opponent and to the judges. The judges include at least one master. He makes sure that everyone is being fair.

To win in sparring, you have to score more points than your opponent. To make a point, you have to kick your opponent hard enough for him to be shaken up by it. Don't worry—you'll both be wearing a lot of padding! You won't get hurt, but you can still be stunned. It is possible to win a point for a punch, but most people get points for their kicks instead—as you know, kicking is much more powerful.

After the match, the master in the jury reads what the judges have decided and tells the referee who the winner is. If you break the rules, you could lose a point or even be disqualified—this means that you lose automatically.

Competitors are divided up by age, belt, and weight. The ages are divided up this way: 6- to 8-year-olds, 9- to 10-year-olds, 11- to 12-year-olds, 13- to 14-year-olds, and 15- to 16-year-olds. Belts are divided by color: yellow, green, blue, and red belts each compete in separate divisions. Black belts are divided only by age (13–16) and weight.

Kyuk Pah (Board-Breaking) Tournaments

The third way to be in a tournament is to compete in board breaking, called kyuk pah in Korean. Kyuk pah is a way for the judges to learn how much power you have. It's hard to tell how much power a kick or punch has just by looking at it. By seeing how many boards you can break, though, the judges have a way to test your power. Kyuk pah is also a way to see how good your techniques are. Some techniques are much easier than others, and the judges are always impressed when someone tries an especially tough breaking technique. Also, if you can do kyuk pah well, you will gain more confidence in yourself.

In all three categories—poomse (forms), kyroogi (sparring), and kyuk pah (board breaking)—the top three winners get a medal. In the State Championships, the top three winners can compete in the National Championships. This is a great honor, and any student who has come this far should feel very proud! Competition is a great way for you to get better in taekwondo, to boost your confidence, and to make many new friends along the way!

eight

THE FIVE AIMS OF TAEKWONDO

While the kicks, blocks, punches, and stances of taekwondo are very important, the philosophy of this martial art is equally important. Remember, a martial art is a way of life, not just a style of fighting. There are five important goals you need to keep in mind when learning taekwondo: respect, humility, perseverance, self-control, and honesty. These are pretty hard concepts to understand, so let's go over them one by one.

RESPECT

When you have respect for a person, including yourself, it means that you have a feeling of honor for them. Someone who respects himself would always act in ways that bring honor to himself, his family, and his friends. One way that taekwondo practitioners show respect to each other is by bowing. (Remember, to bow is kyung nay in Korean.) Respect is one of the most important things you learn in taekwondo. A good taekwondo practitioner shows respect to all people, not just those he or she likes. You will learn that the more you show respect to others, the more they will respect you.

HUMILITY

Being humble about your abilities is another important part of your training. Bragging, showing off, and other types of boasting have no place in the life of anyone who practices taekwondo. This means that you shouldn't try to impress people by telling them about your skill in taekwondo. If you really are a good practitioner, you will not want to say anything to impress people. Many of the finest taekwondo competitors in the world make no mention at all about their abilities.

> *Taekwondo Tip*
>
> **When you become great in taekwondo, you will feel great. You will also come to understand that the people who talk the most about their skills are usually those who understand the least.**

PERSEVERANCE

In taekwondo, you will face many tests. The first, and probably the easiest, is simply getting started in a good dojang. Once you do that, you will begin to learn many new things. Basic stances, blocking, punches, kicks, and a special way of behaving are just some things you will work on with your sabumnim during your first three months of training. You will also learn to listen well and to obey the strict rules of the dojang. At many points along the way, you may feel uncoordinated, tired, and unable to do the things your sabumnim asks of you. It is during these times that you will need to use your perseverance—and everyone has more than they think! It is much easier to give up and quit when you're doing something that's difficult, but if you work a little harder and keep on trying, you'll discover that you really *can* do it! This is perseverance.

> *Taekwondo Tip*
>
> **Taekwondo will put you through some tests that you will never experience elsewhere. If you can pass the tests of taekwondo, then the tests of ordinary life, such as those in school or the ones you face with your friends and family every day, will become much easier.**

SELF-CONTROL

As we discussed before, people who practice taekwondo must set a good example for others. This isn't always easy, especially when there are other kids who might try to talk you into making a decision you know is wrong. A taekwondo practitioner does not get involved with kids like this and doesn't make decisions based on what those kids might think—this is self-control.

Self-control also means staying calm and using your head—not your punches or kicks—when you get upset. While other people might lose control when they are scared or angry, you must stay calm and use your mind to figure out the smartest way to solve to your problem. If someone is bothering you, you do not need to hurt that person. In fact, this would go against the philosophy of taekwondo and would show only weakness on your part. Instead, you might talk to a teacher who knows you, go directly to the principal, or ask your parents to talk to the parents of the boy or girl who is giving you trouble.

By using your mind, you can stay in control of almost any situation. After you've learned this, you can use your confidence and your self-control to achieve the goals you set for yourself. So, not only does self-control help you better handle everyday situations, but it also helps you prepare for your future. This is one of the most important things you will get from your training in taekwondo.

HONESTY

Being honest is very important, especially for a student of taekwondo. In order to get better at taekwondo, you must be honest with yourself about your abilities so that you can figure out what areas you need to work on. This will put you on the right path toward becoming your very best.

You also must be honest with other people, especially your parents, friends, and teachers. If you would like people to trust you, you must give them a reason. If you lie and do not take responsibility for your actions, people will no longer trust you. Even if you were never dishonest again, it would be hard for people to believe that you mean what you say. Therefore, it is very important to behave honorably and to be honest at all times.

Taekwondo can change your life in amazing ways, but only if you work hard and live by the philosophies of the martial art. You will learn new things and face new challenges every time you go to a taekwondo class. It is very important that you attend classes as much as you can. If possible, you should try to show up at least three times a week. If you do this, things like competition and belt tests will become much easier. Training in taekwondo takes lots of hard work. But once you've seen yourself improve and reach the goals you've set for yourself, you'll be a champion in every way, and you'll never want to trade places with anyone!

OTHER BOOKS IN THIS SERIES

ISBN 0-8048-3534-9

ISBN 0-8048-3600-0

ISBN 0-8048-3563-2